Jokes, Toasts and One-liners for Wedding Speeches

Jokes, Toasts and One-liners for Wedding Speeches

Original lines to make them laugh and cry

from **confetti.co.uk**
don't get married without us...

First published in 2004
by Octopus Publishing Group
2–4 Heron Quays
London E14 4JP
www.conran-octopus.co.uk

Written for Confetti by Sticky Content Ltd
Text copyright © 2004 Confetti Network Ltd;
Book design and layout copyright
© 2004 Conran Octopus Ltd;
Illustrations copyright © 2004 Confetti Network Ltd

A catalogue record for this book is available from
the British Library.
ISBN 1 84091 370 3

Publishing Director Lorraine Dickey
Senior Editor Katey Day
Assistant Editor Sybella Marlow
Art Director Chi Lam
Designer Jeremy Tilston
Assistant Production Controller Natalie Moore

Other books in this series include: *How to Write a Wedding
Speech*; *The Best Man's Speech*; *The Best Man's Wedding*;
Wedding Readings; *Wedding Speeches*; *Men at Weddings*
and *The Wedding Book of Calm*

Contents

So you've been asked to give a wedding speech or make a wedding toast. Naturally you're flattered, and it would be rude to refuse – whatever the state of your nerves.

You've probably got a good idea of the structure you want and the tone of voice you're after: irreverently affectionate perhaps, or fondly sentimental, or downright racy. Now all you have to do is work out what to say!

But however long or short you plan your speech to be, however respectful or rude, you'll get nowhere without some decent material. Doubtless you've got your own store of anecdotes and memories to draw on for the heart of your address.

But what's often hardest are those funny little lines that bring an idea alive, those little jokes and witticisms that can keep the laughter count high and the audience on your side.

That's where this handy little book can help. Whether it's an original gag about the groom's bald patch, a light-hearted remark to take everyone's mind off the bad weather, or a sensitive yet humorous way to make a toast on behalf of a dear departed parent, you'll find the right thing to say here.

We've arranged this versatile compendium of jokes and one liners by subject, so whether you want to talk about pets or cars or the groom's outrageous dancing style, you'll never be short of an apt phrase or witty aside. As well as all this, you'll find sample wedding toasts for all situations, and advice on how to make sure your speech goes with a bang!

And so, ladies and gentlemen, without further ado…

How to be funny

Make 'em laugh!

Every speaker wants to raise the roof – or at least a few smiles. Don't feel under pressure to be funny. Remember that everyone's on your side and they want your words to work as much as you do.

• Establish a rapport with your audience by referring to something topical that all present can relate to: 'Phew! I don't know about you but I thought I was going to keel over in that church…'
• Nervous? Don't panic. Make a gag about Imodium or jelly legs! (See under *Nerves* page 68.)
• Try and enjoy yourself – or look like you are. It'll relax the room.
• Keep it simple. If you have to explain the gag, you're doing it wrong!
• Practice makes perfect. Test out your speech on friends and colleagues, note their reactions and amend as necessary.
• Think of your whole audience. Avoid private in-jokes, technical jargon and anything that might offend granny.
• Be sensitive. Avoid referring to previous partners, weight problems, but if you have to, do so with great care. Above all, don't offend the bride. If in doubt, leave it out!
• Be brief. Even the best speech can become a yawn if it goes on too long.
• Jokes aren't everything. Sometimes a few words spoken from the heart can be just as effective.

Timing and delivery

You know what they say: 'The secret of comedy… is… in … the… timing.' And then they say: 'It ain't what you say, it's the way that you say it.' Well, they may be clichés, but they're no less true for all that. Check out these tips:

• Speak clearly. It doesn't matter how great your material is if no one can make out what you're saying.
• Always keep the punchline a surprise. If the end of your joke is 'Five donkeys and a unicorn', make sure you don't mention the keywords 'donkeys' or 'unicorn' in the build-up.
• Take a good long breath between each sentence. Public speakers invariably speed up as they go, and what to you sounds nice and slow may well come over at breakneck speed.
• If you can, check out the venue beforehand. Get someone to stand at the back and make sure that you can be heard.
• If people are laughing, enjoy the ride! Don't try and talk over them.
• Check out any props and equipment you're planning on using. Have an emergency fall-back plan: what will you do if the slide projector/microphone breaks down?
• Treat wedding hecklers with a smile. They're usually good-natured.

What the experts say

'The more you practise delivering your speech, the less nervous you will be. Practise the pauses, the intonations, the anecdotes. By showing you've put even a little thought and effort into what you're saying, all manner of sins will be forgiven. Recite your speech in the shower. On the bus. On the loo. On the night, your nerves will thank you, because instead of fretting about the audience or your flies, you'll simply focus on what you're going to say.'
Rob Pointer, stand-up comic and serial best man

'Don't speak when you're looking down at your notes. Look down for a moment, look up, smile at everyone, speak – then repeat. You don't need to talk constantly; it gives guests a break, and if you're not afraid of silence, you'll look confident, so everyone can relax. Remember that in between speaking, silence feels approximately ten times longer than it is, so take it nice and slow.'
Jill Edwards, comedy coach and scriptwriter

Lines that work – and lines that don't...

Always a winner
'Not for the first time today do I rise from a warm seat clutching a piece of paper...'
'I'm going to make this short and sweet. Thanks very much.' [Speaker sits down.]
'And so without further ado, let's raise our glasses...'
'I'm sure you'll agree that I'm the luckiest man/woman in the world today.'
'I do!'

Definite no-nos
'I wouldn't say the bride looks fat in that dress, but...'
'Turning now to Simon's third marriage...'
'Not being a big fan of marriage myself...'
'When I was going out with the bride/groom...'
'Frankly, I'm amazed we've got this far without my parents coming to blows...'
Any reference to bridal pregnancy (except by prior agreement).
References to the cost of the wedding.

Good for a groan
'Unaccustomed as I am to public speaking...'
'My wife/husband and I...'

A–Z of jokes and one-liners

Stuck for a witticism to fill out your epic speech?
Looking for a rib-tickler or two to break up the
serious/romantic bits with a chortle?

Let our directory of jokes and one-liners, based on
real wedding speeches and toasts, take the strain.
We've arranged this **A–Z** to cover all the subjects that
most commonly come up in a wedding speech –
everything from first impressions to the groom's
sporting prowess.

All you need to do is search for the subject you're
after, or if you're stuck for inspiration, just dip in
and browse. Not every line will fit the speech or
toast you're planning exactly, of course, but
hopefully you'll find an idea you can adapt, a
line you can make your own.

As you prepare your words, remember not to
try too hard. You don't have to be a stand-up to storm
at a wedding, just someone who's put a little time,
care and thought into your speech…

Aaaaagh!

'Tall, handsome, sensitive, intelligent, funny, brave, musical and athletic. I am all these things – so why on earth did Paula have to go and marry Mark?'

Absent friends

'I'd just like to read a text message from Terry, the landlord at The Grapes, where Bob and Carol like to go for a drink on the occasional night with a "y" in it:
"Congratulations to you both. Sorry I can't be there today but work's work, and there's a big crowd in for the football. Everyone sends their love, and the wife asks if you could send us a picture of the beaming bride and groom, mounted." [Pause, then look up] Surely just a peck on the cheek would do?'

'Sadly, Michael/Micha cannot be with us today. But if he/she were here, I know exactly what he/she would say: "Great suit/dress, Bob/Roberta, but £300 for some fancy paper serviettes? ARE YOU OUT OF YOUR MIND?"'

'It's a great shame Colin couldn't be with us tonight, though I know a couple of people – Jack and Jim – who're quite glad he's not, as he always really lays into one of them. Mr Jack Daniels and Mr Jim Beam, that is.'

[Mother of bride standing in for deceased father of bride] 'If my husband were here today, he'd say, "Typical! You never could resist sticking your oar in, could you?" And, of course, he'd be right. But then again, if I can't say my piece today of all days, when can I? Juliet is truly her father's daughter and I know that she's missing him today as much as I am. Weddings are a time of happiness, not sadness, but we both agreed that we couldn't let this occasion pass without dad getting a mention. And now I hear him whispering in my ear: "Get on with it woman!"'

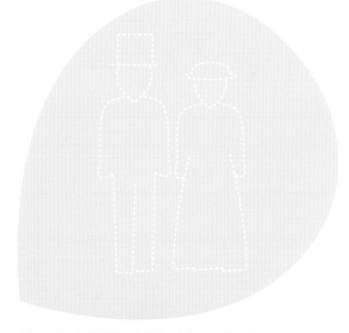

Accidents

'Well, it's certainly been an eventful day already, and full
marks to all the organizers for keeping us on our toes.
The flat battery in the bride's limo was an original start – or
non-start – and the "£5 OFF" stickers clearly visible on the
groom's heels made for a real talking point. The vicar's
uncontrollable hayfever was a truly inspired touch, topped
off by the father of the groom taking two-and-a-half hours
to drive the three miles from the ceremony to the
reception. All in all, it's been a day that no one will forget
in a hurry, and it's these funny little moments that we will
all remember with a smile when we look back on this special
day. At least that's what I keep telling the bride and groom.
Now [feel frantically in all pockets]: where's my speech?'

Age gap

'People often ask us if the age gap between me and Janine has a big impact on our relationship. And I always say [shouting, cupping ear with hand]: "WHAT'S THAT? CAN YOU SPEAK UP, DEAR? YES, LOVELY WEATHER WE'VE BEEN HAVING…"'

'When Tom first asked Emma out, he asked her if she liked Spandau Ballet. She said she preferred the opera…'

'Kate took a keen professional interest in Steve. She's an archaeologist.'

Army

'James did once think of joining the army. But let's face it, the only army he'd join would have a white cross on a white background for its flag…'

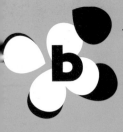

Babies

'Do Fred and Jo want babies? Well, let's just say I know what religion the Pope is and we all know what bears do in the woods…'

Baby memories

'Karen was always a very generous soul, right back to when she was a small child and would gladly share the contents of her potty with whomever was passing. We all got used to it after a while, though I'm not sure the postman ever did.'

Bad habits

'In a world without women, you'd be served smaller portions in restaurants. That's because you wouldn't have to fend off the dive-bomb raids from the vulture by your side who's just told the waiter she's not hungry but who, now she's set her beady eyes on your grub, is suddenly absolutely ravenous. And yes, I'm talking about you, Nicky.'

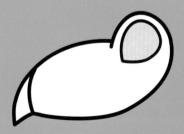

'[In spoof policeman's voice, perhaps wearing copper's helmet and consulting notebook] Now then, now then, has Steve got a record of bad habits, you ask? Indeed he has, I'm afraid, and it's a most criminal one. He's done time for hoarding old bus tickets and nibbling his toenails; when it comes to loo seats he's a persistent repeat offender; and he's also asked for 27 cases of mouldy sock abuse to be taken into consideration...'

Bathroom habits
'I won't say that Lyn likes to spend a long time getting ready in the bathroom, but usually by the time I've waited for her to come out, I need to shave again.'

'Though he is generally very good at technical stuff, Graeme has little understanding of the science behind dandruff or the hidden causes of the split end. This is a man who scrubs his scalp every night with Ajax and a Brillo pad.'

'I'm told that Jeremy always likes to listen to a Wagner opera or two while on the loo. "Why's that?" I asked. "Because you're guaranteed several movements," he replied.'

Bedroom

'And here is a picture of Tom's room when he was a child...'
[Display a picture of an enormous, seagull-riddled rubbish tip
on a flipchart or slide projector]

'When I went round to Eve's place for the first time
and saw her room, two words popped into my mind:
"Landfill site."'

Beginnings

[Adopt mock-solemn expression, then say as you make
the sign of the cross] 'In the name of the father and the
son and the... [pause, look confused] Oh no. Sorry.
We've done that bit.'

[Adopt northern accent of old-style comic] 'Now here's
another one you won't get: Why does a cucumber make a
better lover than the mother-in-law? [Pause] 'Oh sorry.
Wrong gig.'

Beginnings

'Brevity, as I explain on page 72 of my speech, is indeed the soul of wit.'

'I've been told the essence of a good speech is to stand up and be seen, speak up and be heard, and sit down and shut up.' [Sit down]

[Said by speaker with bald hair or receding hairline]
'I've been really worried about this speech. So worried, in fact, that I've been tearing my hair out.'

Best man

'I'm told that one of the few acceptable reasons for turning down the job of best man is when you don't know the groom that well and are not even really sure why you've been asked. Well nothing could be further from the case with me and Eric... I mean, Bert... I mean Steve...'

'They say that when it comes to the best man's speech the guests are usually nice and warmed up by all the booze and the sentimental speeches that have gone before. I just hope it doesn't get so warm that it brings the tumbleweed out...'

'And now, let me hand you over to my vest man, I mean my best man, Eddie...'

Birthdays

'Today, for those of you who don't know, it also happens to be the father of the bride's birthday. What rotten luck – having to buy everyone the first round at the bar on top of everything else he's spent today!'

'As some of you may know, today is my birthday. At the risk of sounding corny, let me just say that my new wife/husband is the best present anyone could wish for.'

Bride's father

[Speaking of groom] 'It's customary for the father of the bride to say on a day like today that he and his wife haven't so much lost a daughter as gained a son. Well, in our case, we haven't so much lost a daughter as gained an obsessive Wolves fan with an unusually large collection of cowboy boots and an old Triumph Herald in pieces all over our back garden!'

Cars
'And here – ah, this one takes me back…
[Display picture of rubbish-filled skip on flipchart or slide projector] Here's a picture of Garry's first car.'

Childhood
'When Jane was only 11, she took up the trombone. And once we'd heard her practising, we made sure she'd given it up by 11.30.'

Children
'I'd like to say a big thank you to my one-year-old nephew Paul, without whose constant help and attention this wedding would have been prepared in half the time.'

Children from previous relationships
'Blimey. I knew that both Jeff and Deanne already had family [shield your eyes as you scan the assembled guests, then say incredulously:] But surely you can't all be their children!'

Chocolate

'Chocoholic Mary is quite the philosopher. Ask her the secret of a happy and healthy life, and she'll say: "A Mars a day helps you work, rest and play." Ask her for her solution to today's rising stress levels, and she'll say, "Have a break, have a Kit Kat." And ask her about what attracted her to Barry and she'll say: [sing it, if you dare…] "EVERYONE'S A FRUIT AND NUT CASE!"'

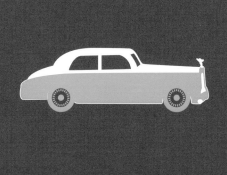

College

'As students, Rob and I were paupers. We used to make a teabag last a week. We ate tomato ketchup sandwiches. We went to the public loo over the road because we couldn't afford to buy loo roll. And once, we nicked a load of food from the kitchen of a party because we had nothing to eat the next day. Rob stood at the top of the stairs while I lobbed him down crisps and groceries. "Quick," I whispered. "Put these sardines in your pocket."

"I can't." Rob whispered back desperately.

"Oh come on – this is no time to get moral," I snapped.

"It's not that," said Rob. "It's just I've got half-a-dozen eggs in there already. And I've just sat on one".'

Compatibility

'Of course, Alan and Chloe have both had partners before, but neither has really found anyone totally compatible. Who else would be prepared to lend a hand when Alan cleans out his salamander tank? And who else would be prepared to cheer and sing as Chloe shows off her newly choreographed routine to Barry Manilow's "*Copacabana*"?'

'In the little-known Cockney horoscope, Darren was born in the Year of the Jellied Eel, while Siobhan was born in the Year of the Potted Shrimp. This is always a very happy combination because eels are electric on the dance floor, and Siobhan was tickled pick when he brought her out of her shell. Prawn again, she was…'

Cooking

'It's not that Justin is a particularly bad cook, but the cockroaches in the kitchen have just asked for a suggestion box.'

'Tim insists that all those pungent dishes he slaves over for hours in the kitchen are "100 per cent cruelty-free". I don't know about that. I reckon his mushroom risotto could do a bit of damage in the wrong hands!'

Culture

'As you know, Terry is a bit of a class act. He thinks "erudite" is a glue, spells culture with a "K", orders his steak tartare "well done", sends his crème brûlée back when it arrives burnt, and thinks the London Underground is a dangerous political movement. And when he was asked if he was going to wear his morning suit today, he replied: [adopt gormless tone] "Why? Who's died?"'

Dancing
'On the stag night I came across two of our mates, Kev and Ian, with bleeding noses. "Have you two been fighting?" I asked anxiously. "Nah," they said. "We got these dancing next to Gary!"'

Décor
'If you've ever been round to Simone and George's, you'll know that the bathroom has been done out in a charming aquatic theme. There are sea horses on the shower curtains, sea shells on the aquamarine walls, and loofahs and sponges everywhere you look. It's all a matter of taste, of course, but the goldfish in the bidet seemed a bit OTT to me…'

Degree
'Janine is always one to hide her light under a bushel. Many of you may not know, for instance, that at college she was the author of a ground-breaking paper entitled: Symbolism and the Alarm Clock, 1912–56/The Reproductive Cycle of the Common Termite/Metaphor and Simile in Dynasty.'

Dieting

'Caroline has been planning her wedding for as long as anyone can remember. In fact, she's been on her special "Wedding Dress Diet" since 1994. Which is odd, as she only met Gary in 1997…'

Differences between husband and wife

'Pam and Pete are very different characters, but they say opposites attract and in their case that's certainly true. To get an idea of their chalk-cheese relationship, ask them to sit down on the sofa and then shout: "OOH AAH!" Pete will jump up and start shouting, "OOH AAH CANTONAAAA!" Pam, meanwhile, will start dancing and singing: "OOH AAH JUST A LITTLE BIT! OOH AAH A LITTLE BIT MORE!"'

DIY

'Paul is so keen on DIY that he once turned up at a fancy dress party attached to a long piece of wood on which he had placed three cans of lager, a clock, an ashtray and a copy of *High Fidelity*. "What on earth is that?" I asked, pointing to his outfit. Paul replied: "I'VE COME AS MY SHELF!"'

Drinking habits

'I wouldn't say Louisa has a drinking problem but I did once catch her trying to down a bottle of aftershave. "What on earth are you doing that for?" I asked. "I thought it was *eau de cologne*," she replied.

'George is certainly a fixture down at his local in the village. You know you're a valued customer when the landlord's sheepdog will cash cheques for you!'

Driving

'It would be unfair to describe Charlie as the world's worst driver. There's a getaway driver on *Police! Cameras! Action!* who'd give him a good run for his money.'

'Once I gave Dave a call as he was driving home from work on the ring road. "Be careful," I said. "Apparently, there's some nutter who's driving in the wrong direction." "It's not just one," said Dave. "There's blooming hundreds of them."'

'Pauline's legendary short-sightedness didn't really help when it came to her driving test. "I want you to pull out after that red van, then stop when you see the Give Way sign," said the instructor. So Pauline replied: [put on panicky voice] "WHO SAID THAT?!"'

'Jemima very kindly gave me a lift to the wedding rehearsal yesterday. "Can I drop you outside?" she asked. "Yeah, that's great," I said. "I can walk to the kerb from here!"'

'Once, when Jason and I were driving down the M1, we had a heated debate about party politics. Jason, who was driving, asked me who I voted for and I said, rather loudly, "Middle of the road!"
"There's nothing wrong with that," said Jason. "Why the terrified look?"
"No," I said. "LOOK OUT, WE'RE DRIVING IN THE CENTRAL RESERVATION!"'

Eating habits

'The first time I had dinner with Eric I couldn't quite work out where I'd seen his eating habits before. It wasn't until the following weekend, when I took my little niece to see the monkeys being fed at the zoo…'

Endings

'Well, that's it from me. If you liked my speech, the name's ___ [give your name]. If you didn't, it's ___ [give the name of another speaker, such as the best man].'

'And, finally, I'd like to finish with a big thank you to all of those who managed to stay awake during my speech and even to laugh politely in one or two places. In fact, you've been such a lovely audience I only wish I'd had better material…'

'Ups and downs, high and lows, an emotional rollercoaster, in sickness and in health. And that's just my speech!'

'And finally: Confucius, the Chinese philosopher, says something very profound about the secret essence of a truly happy and harmonious marriage. But it was in Chinese, unfortunately, so I never quite got it. Instead, let me simply ask you to be upstanding as we toast…'

Engagement

'I'll never forget the night when Josh called to say: "I'm engaged!" I replied: "Well, call me back when you're off the loo." [pause] Sorry, ladies and gentlemen, that joke was complete toilet. What a loo-ser…' [continue with as many gags in a similar vein as you dare…]

'The day after I said "yes" to Tom, he called me up at three in the morning. "I told you I'd give you a ring," he said.'

'I wouldn't say my parents were "pleasantly surprised" when I told them that Jean had accepted my hand in marriage. "Pleasantly gobsmacked" would be much more like it.'

'It wasn't that Frances took a bit of persuading to marry Ashley. Unless you count asking her 14 times "a bit of persuading". Come to think of it, when she finally accepted, he did send an email round to friends and family with the headline: "GOTCHA!"'

'As many of you will know, Tony and I have been engaged for no less than 3/7/9 years. You're probably wondering: Was it worth the wait? Well, ask me after the honeymoon. We're due back in August... 2047.'

'James and Belinda have been engaged for so long that I shall now read the following congratulatory telemessage from the Queen...'

Exes

[NB: Previous partners are a very sensitive subject, so tread carefully. If in doubt, avoid. If you do think it's safe to include a line, why not make a joke about an imaginary ex rather than a real person, talk about a childhood sweetheart, or say something general about how the bride or groom never found anyone who was just right before?]

'I'm not saying Jo's first boyfriend wasn't marriage material, but on his forehead he'd tattooed the word "OOTATT."'

'It's not the done thing to say too much about exes in a wedding speech, I know, but I think that we should all spare a thought for June's former boyfriend Robbie. Robbie and June used to be inseparable. They'd go out for long cycle rides together, drink from the same straw, hold hands in the park. But, unfortunately, they split up over a tragic incident in which Robbie spilt paint over June's favourite outfit. She was the only girl in her class to have dungarees, and in all my life I've never seen a seven-year-old girl quite so upset.'

Father of the bride

'It's been an absolute pleasure to give away my daughter today. My only regret is that I didn't do it years ago…'

First boyfriend/girlfriend

'Dan's first girlfriend, when he was seven, was called Sarah. Her dad, Mr Taylor, used to run the clock shop up the road, so Dan's family called her Sarah "Tick Tock" Taylor. Unfortunately, she fell out with him when he tried to bribe her with a pencil sharpener to see up her skirt. They've not seen each other for 20 years but tonight, ladies and gentlemen, thanks to the power of the internet, HERE SHE IS… [make a big gesture and point to the nearest door, as if she's about to walk in, then pause, as nothing happens] No, not really.'

First date

'The first time Jerry and I went out on a date, he clearly
wanted to make a big impression. The pub he took us
to was so rough that even the arms on the chairs had
tattoos. There was a trivia quiz on that night and the first
question was: "Who d'you think you're looking at, mush?"
The tie-breaker was: "Who spilled my pint?" After that,
we went to a club round the corner. The bouncer asked:
"Have you got any offensive weapons?"
"Of course not," we replied. So he handed us some broken
bottles and said: "You'd better take these. It's gets pretty
nasty in here."'

First impressions

'The first time I met my future parents-in-law, I choked on
a tea cake, stepped on the cat and smashed a French window
as the result of an over-energetic game of swingball. But it
wasn't all plain sailing. Let me tell you about some of the
sticky moments…'

First time we met

'The first time I met Greg, at a party, he was 17. He leaned over, looked up at me with his big blue eyes, smiled...
then threw up on my shoe. Then he uttered those immortal words which I shall never forget: "Got a fag?" In that heart-stopping moment, somehow, I just knew. So help me God, I knew.'

[After a protracted engagement] 'I knew at once that I had made a big impression on Cath, because shortly after that first fateful meeting, she went and left the country for three months/started dating my flatmate/converted to Christianity/joined Narcotics Anonymous/took to meditating every night/did a First Aid course!'

Fishing

'The first time I stayed over at Miles's, I asked what he liked doing to relax. He said: "Night fishing." Well, I'd never heard it called that before!'

Football

'Adam is so football-mad that it took us weeks to persuade him not to have the wedding list at the Arsenal gift shop [pause]. We were particularly against the idea as we'd already spent a weekend there on the stag do.'

[Bride speaking] 'In the run-up to this wedding, I found a good way of calming my nerves was to adopt one of those New-Age affirmations, and repeat it over and over again every day like a mantra. I chose: "Every day, in every way, I am getting closer to the wedding of my dreams." I found it really helpful and said to Adam that if he felt nervous he should think up an affirmation, too. Then one night I heard him talking to himself in the bath. I put my ear to the bathroom door, and heard him saying over and over again: "Every day, in every way, Brighton are getting closer to the play-offs."'

'As I got to know Paul and his family, I noticed that he and his dad observed a religious ritual every Saturday afternoon, at exactly twenty to five. The house would fall silent and all would gather around a bright box in the corner of the living room to worship and give praise. That's right, you guessed it, it was *Final Score*.'

'The other night I went for a meal round at Ian and Martha's. I couldn't help noticing that there were about a dozen salt and pepper pots spread out on the kitchen table. "What are all those for?" I asked. "I'm still trying to explain to Martha the offside rule," said Ian.

'I couldn't help noticing during the service that the best man kept passing the father of the bride little folded-up pieces of paper. After a while, I got a bit curious, so when the next one came over I intercepted it and opened it up. It said: "Tranmere 3, Rotherham 2".'

Friendship

'As I said to my parents last night, the best thing is that today I am marrying my best friend. I don't know where I'd be without… er, whatisname, you know…'

Funny habits

'If it weren't for people like Sally, video players would be made without the pause button. This is because there would no longer be any need to stop the film to run through the plot again every ten minutes!'

'As a child, Laura was so absent-minded, she was the only paying member of the town library!'

Gardening

'You can sum up the progress of green-fingered Jack and Jane's relationship in these three emails, which I received from Jack over a period of six months:
1 "Can't make the pub tonight – am going on a date with a fantastic girl I just met."
2 "Can't make the footie – I'm whisking Jane off to Barcelona for the weekend."
And finally:
3 "Can't make the barbecue Saturday – we've got a serious mulch situation."'

Golf

'Golf is certainly Pete's passion. Possibly his only one. The other night, as we were enjoying an intimate moment, I'm sure I heard him call out: "SEVE!"'

'Golf has been a passion of mine for as long as I can remember, but I'm afraid that June's never really got into it. The one time she came along, as she landed in a bunker for the third hole running, I asked her if she wanted a sand wedge. She said: "Ooooh lovely – have you got any tuna and cucumber?"'

Gossip

'Now Ginny loves gossip. When Rupert started working
in her office, she was the first to find out where he lived,
where he'd worked previously, what he thought of his boss
and whether he had a girlfriend. He said he was single;
she showed him otherwise.'

Guests

'It'll be easy to spot any gatecrashers today: they'll be the
ones laughing at the jokes in my speech!'

'I'm afraid I've mislaid the actual text of my speech, so
instead I'll be taking questions from the audience...'
[You could use this as an introductory joke, then miraculously
find the piece of paper, or you could actually turn your
speech into a series of answers to questions that you
will have carefully planted with guests beforehand.]

'If anyone can see any way that I can still get out of giving
this speech, speak now or forever hold your peace...'

Gullible

'I wouldn't say Dan's taken in by advertising, but for years
he wouldn't order Strongbow because he didn't want to get
shot by an arrow. He thought Dr Pepper was a real doctor,
always ate his sweetcorn because he was afraid of the Jolly
Green Giant, and once almost came a cropper trying to
ride an egg to work.'

Hair

'Jim's so bald that the last time he went to the barbers and asked for a number three, they told him to come back in a year's time when it had grown.'

'I wouldn't say Dave's obsessed with his barnet, but he's just had his car fitted with a hair-view mirror.'

Handsome

'The groom didn't always look as good as he does today. When he was born the midwife took one look at him and slapped his father. His mum pushed the only pram in town with shutters. And when she fed him, she used a catapult!'

'That's funny. I thought Paul said he was going to wait till after he was married before he really let himself go.'

'Gary was quite a big lad when he was younger, as I was reminded when he showed me some old school photos recently. "Goodness me," I said. "You were really tubby!" Gary said, "Yes, but don't forget the camera adds several pounds!" I replied: "God – so how many cameras were on you that day?!"'

'Simon has a beautiful nose. He picked it himself. He took it apart once to see what made it run.'

Hen night

'Hen nights are a great time for the girls to get together and let their hair down, discuss their real feelings about marriage and relationships, and have a good old moan about the lads. Our night had quite a hippie feel for some reason, with everyone talking about good vibrations. Or something like that.'

Holidays

'Travelling abroad can often be a very stressful time for couples, but as Trudy and Joe prepare to jet off on their honeymoon to Sardinia, they can at least relax in the knowledge that they have travelled together many times before. There was the time they went Interailing and had to return home after three days when Joe, a little the worse for wear, fell asleep in the middle of a roundabout and had his stuff nicked. He was known for years after as "The man who thought money-belts weren't sexy."'

Honeymoon

'Jake likes to really unwind on holiday, but I hope he won't get too relaxed on his honeymoon with Jill. I know, from all the rugby tours I've been on with him, that his idea of "relaxing" is not having to get out of the bath to pee.'

'I'm sure that tonight, the start of their honeymoon, Marie and Vic won't make the same mistake as the couple I heard about who slipped away from the reception supper and took some Champagne up to their room. The bride pulled up a chair and sat staring at the stars. After a while her new husband asked: "Aren't you coming to bed, darling?" "NO WAY," she replied. "My mum told me this would be the most beautiful night of my entire life, and I'm not going to miss a second."'

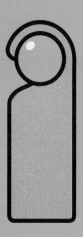

'"Where would you like to go for our honeymoon?"
I asked Tom. He said: "I'd like to go somewhere dangerous
and exciting that I've never been before." So I took him
for a decent haircut!'

'Two eggs are on their honeymoon. In the hotel bedroom,
the couple start canoodling on the bed. Then Mrs Egg gets
up and says to her new husband, "Just wait a moment,
darling. I'm going to go into the bathroom to freshen up
and slip into something more comfortable." A few minutes
later she's back, her smooth oval curves now wrapped in
an eggs-tremely revealing egg-ligée. Mr Egg takes one look
at his beautiful bride, looks startled and claps his hands over
the top of his head. "What are you doing that for, darling?"
his wife asks. He replies: "Because the last time I was this
egg-cited, someone smacked me over the head with a spoon."

Horoscope

'In the Chinese calendar, Ian comes under the Year of the
Rooster, while Helen was born in the Year of the Ox.
Apparently this makes them "a practical pair who trust
each other completely. The rooster brings out the best in
the shy ox, while the ox provides a calming environment that
soothes the frantic rooster." I doubt if there's anything in it,
but what I do know is that these two should definitely stay
indoors on Bonfire Night.'

Housework

'In our house, I promise my wife here and now, before
everyone present, that I will not treat "wash", "cook" and
"iron" as four-letter words.'

In-laws

'In Dave and Pippa I have gained the perfect in-laws. I always cringe when I hear jokes about difficult mothers-in-law because my own experience has been so far from that stereotype. [Pause, turn to in-laws timorously] Did I read that right?'

Interests

'Eve is obsessed with India. On our first date we went to a Bollywood karaoke bar, and on our second to the latest Bollywood film. I've promised her that I will help her fulfil her dream of visiting the Taj Mahal. I don't care how much it costs: it's the best restaurant in Peckham and it's worth every penny...'

'Until I met Liam, I wasn't really sure that marquetry/basket-weaving/website design could ever really be interesting. But after one conversation with him I was absolutely certain. It definitely isn't.'

'I could never work out why Gordon was so into stamp collecting, and he told me he did it for the ladies. "How come?" I asked. Said Gordon: "Because philately will get you anywhere."'

'Cole is an obsessive stamp collector but, quite understandably perhaps, he didn't talk about his hobby directly in the first few months that we went out together. So for a long time I laboured under the illusion that I had a rival for Cole's love by the name of Penny Black.'

'Jen loves everything to do with keepfit: water aerobics, spinning, pilates, cross-training, step aerobics… you name it, she does it. When we started living together, I soon discovered that we had rather different ideas of what constitutes a "Sunday morning workout".'

Jobs

'Ever the salesman, Kev talked Wendy into marrying him by offering a discount for bulk (he's certainly got the stomach for it) and a buy-now-pay-later deal. And pay later she certainly will. Wendy, for her part, turned down his two-for-one offer but fully intends to hold him to his guarantee of absolute satisfaction. I just hope she's kept the receipt!'

'On behalf of all my colleagues here today, I would like to say that there is no truth in the rumour that actuaries are people who found accountancy too exciting.'

'OK, so during the week my bride/Dad/husband/best man works as a tax inspector/journalist/estate agent/traffic warden. But I'm glad to say that he/she is here today in his/her off-duty capacity as a blushing bride/proud father/loving human being…'

Jokes

'A woman takes her beloved canary to the vet's for an operation. Sadly, the bird dies on the table. But when the vet tells the woman the bad news, she refuses to accept it. "I demand that you check again just to make sure," she says. Next thing she knows, a cat strolls into the surgery, jumps onto the table, sniffs the canary up and down, makes a loud meow, and walks out again. Before the woman can say anything a big golden labrador bounces in, leaps on to the table, licks the bird all over, gives a loud howl, then bounces out again. The vet says to the woman: "I'm afraid the bird is definitely dead. And here is your bill for £250." The woman is flabbergasted. "A bill for £250! What's that for?"

"Well," says the vet, "Normally it wouldn't cost anything like that much. But with the CAT scan and the lab test…"

'A man walks into a dentist's and says: "You've got to help me. I think I'm a moth." The dentist says: "To be quite frank, I don't think I can help. What you need is a psychiatrist. Why did you come in here anyway?" The man replies: "Well, the light was on."'

'A man walks into a doctor's surgery completely wrapped in clingfilm. "Before you say anything," says the doctor, "I can clearly see you're nuts!"'

'A naughty inflatable student is summoned to see the inflatable headmaster of an inflatable school. "That drawing pin incident," the headmaster began. "Not only have you let yourself down, you've let me down, you've let the whole school down."'

'Two women meet at a party. "Isn't your ring on the wrong finger?" asks one. "I know," says the other. "I married the wrong man."'

'What do you call a sheep with no legs?
A cloud.'

'Husband: "Why do you keep studying the wedding licence?"
Wife: "I'm looking for loopholes."'

'A little girl spies her pregnant mum and asks her why her
tummy is so big. "There's a baby in there," says her mum.
"Where did it come from?" asks the little girl, persistently.
"Daddy gave it to me." So the little girl goes and sees her
dad. "Daddy, Daddy," she says. "You know that baby
you gave to Mummy?"
"Yeees," says Dad, a little embarrassed. "Well," sighs the little
girl, "She's only gone and eaten it."'

'Mrs Werewolf: "Hello dear, how was your day?"
Mr Werewolf (just home from work, very moody):
"Leave me alone! I don't want to talk about it!!"
Mrs Werewolf (spotting full moon out of the window):
"Oh dear. Is it that time of the month again already?"'

Kissing

'Seeing the bride and groom exchanging their first kiss as husband and wife today, I'm reminded of the artist who became so attracted to his model that he rushed round from behind his easel, grabbed her in his arms and kissed her passionately. "Maybe your other models let you kiss them!" stormed the model. "But not me!" The artist looked hurt and said: "But I've never kissed a model before." "Really?" she replied, softening a little. "And how many have there been?" "Four," he replied. "An orange, two apples and a banana."'

Before Henry's first date with Emma, he rang me up. "How do I know when to make the first move?" he asked nervously. "Just kiss her when she least expects it," I replied. Next time I saw him he was sporting a swollen eye. "What happened?" I asked. "Did you remember to kiss her when she least expects it?". There was a pause. "Oh" he said. "I thought you said where…"'

Living together

'Mary has done a fine job of turning Thierry from a scruffy, unreliable couch potato into a decent loving adult male human being. Her theory is that men are like wines. They start off as grapes, and it's our job to stomp on them a bit, then keep them in the dark till they mature. And hopefully they'll end up turning into something halfway palatable that you wouldn't mind having dinner with.'

'Daisy has a little prayer she says whenever Brian is getting too much for her. "Lord, give me the wisdom to understand my man. Give me love so I can forgive him. Give me patience to cope with his moods. But please, Lord, don't give me strength or I'll give him the beating of his life."'

'Some mornings I wake up grouchy. And some mornings I just let him/her sleep in!'

'Having cohabited for several years, Karen and Jason have come to an understanding. She doesn't let him smoke in bed, and he doesn't let her sleep in ashtrays.'

Love

'In the beautiful words of Helen Rowland, "Falling in love consists merely of uncorking the imagination and bottling the common sense."'

'Love is… seeing Jodie go along to Peter's morris dancing displays and keeping a straight face all the way through.'

'Love is… seeing Peter trying to look like he's really enjoying himself as he struggles through Jodie's Tuscan risotto that she can never quite make like her mum used to.'

'After we'd been going out for about six months, I whispered to Tom that I loved him. [Pause] Well, I could hardly bring myself to shout it out loud.'

'"The most important thing a father can do for his children is to love their mother," said Henry Ward Beecher. But a burger and fries from time to time is almost as good.'

'"To love," as someone once said, "is to catch a glimpse of heaven." And looking at Cath and Dom's radiant expressions, I think we've all caught a bit of that divine radiance today. [pause, cough] Either that, or my flu's coming back/my trifle's repeating on me.'

'Love may be blind, but marriage is a real eye-opener.'

'Getting older doesn't stop you from loving. But loving can stop you growing old at heart!'

'Today is the perfect day to celebrate the fact that Kylie and Darren, who met in a revolving door three years ago, are still going round together!'

'For better or worse, for richer and poorer, in sickness and in health. Love and marriage are all about sticking together through thick and thin. That reminds me of the joke about the man who spends nights sleeping by his wife's bedside when she falls sick. When she finally comes round, the wife says: "You're always there for me in the bad times. When I got fired, you were a shoulder to lean on. When my business went under, you were a real rock. When we lost the house, you stood by my side. When the car got all smashed up, you gave me your shoulder to lean on. And here you are again, visiting me every day in the hospital. In fact, come to think about it, you bring me nothing but bad luck!"'

'I can say with absolute confidence that Chris and Isabelle will never go the way of a couple I know where the man completely let himself go. One night, his wife said to him: "I can't stand living with you. You leave the place like a pig sty, you wear the same dirty clothes all the time, you never have a bath. Just looking at you puts me off my food." "If it's that bad, why don't you just leave?" says the man dejectedly. "I will," says the woman. "As soon as I've lost another 12 pounds."'

'What's the difference between lust, love and marriage? It's love when your eyes meet across a crowded room. It's lust when your tongues meet across a crowded room. And it's marriage when your belt doesn't meet across a crowded waistline!'

Marriage

'Gabby said that when she grew up she wanted to marry the boy next door. [Pause] She wasn't allowed to cross the road.'

'As you may know, the best man is currently single. He's in the enviable position of being able to marry anyone he pleases; all he's got to do now is find one he pleases. In fact, more and more women are choosing not to get married; he knows this, because they've all told him. He's looking for a woman who'll be able to take a joke. Well, it's the only kind he'll get...'

'What's the wife of a hippy called? Mississippi.'

'This marriage really is the perfect match. She likes jogging and he's on the run from the law.'

'Marriage is a kind of friendship recognized by the police.'

'In the words of Groucho Marx, "Marriage is a wonderful institution, but who wants to live in an institution?"'

'A good marriage is like a holiday. You never want it to end.'

'A good marriage is like a cup of coffee: warm and rich, and sometimes keeps you up all night.'

'One of the great things about marriage is that when you fall out of love with him/her – as will occasionally happen to even the most devoted of couples – marriage keeps you going till you fall back in love again.'

'The happy couple are the perfect match. She's a geologist and he's on the rocks!'

Morning dress

'It's been great – if highly unusual – to see the best man and all the ushers dressed up in morning suits today. And if any of the bridesmaids are available and chocoholics, just think of the old advertising slogan, "P-p-p-p-pick up a penguin."'

Mothers-in-law

'What can I tell you about Paula? So fond am I of my mother-in-law, in fact, that I barely consider her to be my mother-in-law at all…'

Moving in

'When Bettina moved in with Serge, his horizons expanded. Suddenly he was ushered into a whole new world with a strange language and bizarre implements. He was initiated into the mysteries of combination skin and cleansing milk, eyelash curlers and cuticle removers. He learnt that straightening irons have nothing to do with golf, that 'exfoliator' is not a Schwarzenegger film, and that self-depilation doesn't make you blind or put hair on your hands.'

Mum

'Before he had the chance in a million of bumping into Louise at a conference, Dom used to complain that he'd spent his whole life looking for his soulmate but never found anyone who came close. "Well you're never going to find her down at Blockbuster Video or KFC," his mum said.'

'Possibly the only person more delighted to see me get married today is my mum. When I was single and I went to a friend's wedding, she'd ask me all about it afterwards. Then, slowly clearing away the tea things, she'd say something like, "She must have been so proud, the groom's mother." The chin starts to wobble slightly. And then: "I only hope I'm still around when – if – you ever get married." Thanks for not putting on the pressure, mum!'

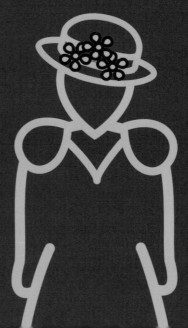

'I'd like to thank my mum for putting up with me over the last few weeks and months, and for all her help in organizing every last little detail of this very special day. And I don't care what she says: she really does have eight pairs of hands!'

'Last night John was staying at his mum's and woke up with a bit of a pain in a delicate place. "Let's have a look," says John's mum. "Come on, I've seen worse – I've seen it all before." "Are you sure?" says John. "Course I have," she says. "I've still got the pictures from when you were a New Romantic."'

Music
'Now, at the risk of shocking some of you, I feel obliged to report that Cameron has a criminal record. He's got several in fact: *The Oldest Swinger in Town, Black Lace's Greatest Hits*, the original score of *Yentl*...'

Names

'I understand that Sophie has agreed to take Andy's unpronounceable surname. Let's hope she never lets on where she's hidden it.'

Neighbours

'A man hears some noise coming from next door's garden. He looks over the fence and sees his neighbour digging furiously. "What are you up to?" he asks. "I'm digging a hole for my canary," says the neighbour. "That's a big hole for a canary, isn't it?" says the man. "Not when it's in your cat," the neighbour replies.'

Nerves

'I'd like to say a big thank you to Alka Seltzer and Imodium, my speech co-sponsors.'

'Does anyone mind if I do this sitting down? Only my legs appear to have turned to jelly.'

'Normally I'm a terrible public speaker, but I'm so proud to see my son/daughter/best friend/brother get married today that I can barely summon a single nerve!'

'I slept like a babe last night. I woke up crying every half an hour, screaming for my mum.'

[At start of speech] 'And so, ladies and gentleman, will you please charge your glasses, and rise and join me… in the pub next door. This speech lark is far too pressurized: I'm going for a pint.'

New man

'I'll never forget the day Anne told me I was going to marry her...'

'John claims to be a new man. He says that once he's married, he's going to take on 50 per cent of all the household chores and shopping, and when the time comes, 50 per cent of all the childcare duties, too. The only things that could possibly get in the way of these noble sentiments are: his allergy to Domestos, the fact that he can't tie his own shoelaces – let alone wipe someone else's bum – oh, and his six-year stretch for perjury.' [At this point, you could have a heckler planted who shouts: 'He told me it was only four!']

Newlyweds

'I'm sure I speak for everyone when I say how much we all wish Penny and Tim a long and happy future together, although I'm not sure it's a good sign that she keeps going round introducing Tim as "my first husband."'

Nocturnal habits

'The other night, unable to sleep because of the noise coming from a certain person not a million miles from here, I sat up late watching an old black-and-white film of *The Ten Commandments*. "Dave's snoring!" I said to myself. "It's enough to wake the dead."
"Tell me about it," says Moses, all of a sudden. "What do you think I'm doing up at this hour?'

'Why do black widow spiders kill their males after mating? To stop the snoring before it starts.'

'In today's politically correct climate, I wouldn't like to say that Stan has a snoring problem. He is, perhaps, a trifle nocturnally challenged. Thankfully he doesn't live in Massachusetts, where snoring is prohibited unless all bedroom windows are closed and securely locked. Or in Canada, where it's grounds for divorce… Fortunately Myra has already found a solution to this little problem. It involves a piece of string, a golf ball, and a strong desire to keep hold of one's privates!'

Office life

'Jeanette was immediately attracted to Brian when they met at work because of his wild, devil-may-care attitude. Indeed, Brian was such a maverick that he could sometimes be seen doing photocopies with the lid up – in full view of the boss! And, occasionally, he would even turn up for work wearing socks of a light grey or tan shade. Well, on Dress Down Fridays. Well, sometimes.'

Outfits

'Geena has had a strong influence on Terry's wardrobe. Gone are the Mr Men socks, the Dangermouse ties, the Team Ferrari sleeveless bodices and, for Christmas, his unforgettable Rudolph the Red Nose Reindeer knitwear. Terry's loss is the world's gain.'

'As you may or may not know, Samantha is obsessed with the colour purple. She's got purple wellies, a purple car, purple kitchen roll and purple bedroom walls. You won't believe the fight we had to get her into a white dress today!'

Pets

'Remember, Judy: a husband's not just for Christmas...'

'When she was little, Simone always wanted a pony. But how times have changed! Today she wouldn't get out of bed for less than a couple of monkeys...'

'The French often say of the British that they prefer animals to humans, and if they met Betty, they'd find plenty of ammunition for their argument. Betty keeps a picture of her border collie, Jamie, on her desk at work; she employs a full-time rota of (heavily-vetted!) dog-sitters; and once even considered hiring a pet psychotherapist to cope with Jamie's mood swings. But let me just put it on record, once and for all: there is NO TRUTH in the rumour that Betty told the girls on her hen night that Jamie kisses better than her new husband!'

Politics

'Polly and I fell out early on over politics. She asked me in a restaurant if I was a Blairite. I replied that I'd always preferred Una Stubbs. Then she asked me what I thought of Cherie, and I said I'd sometimes have a glass with my mum at Christmas...'

Popping the question

'I'll never forget it. It was a beautiful summer's evening, the birds were singing and a cool breeze was gently ruffling Cath's silken tresses. The moment was perfect. My heart was in my mouth as I leaned over and whispered in her ear. "Cath," I said, trembling, "Don't you think it's time we... got Sky Sports/laid some decking in the garden/bought a microwave?"'

'We were on a romantic weekend break, in Barcelona. As we sat outside by the marina after a wonderful seafood meal with loads of wine, James gazed into my eyes and – in a slightly slurred voice – said the immortal words: "Monica, will you carry me?"'

Preparations

'This has been the best organized wedding I've ever attended. Never before have I been to a wedding where the bats in the belfry are wearing corsages, or where five vicars were rejected because their eye colour didn't coordinate with the bridal dress. And when one of the ushers complained of feeling "a bit green around the gills" this morning, he was told it was the wrong shade of green and made to go and have three stiff whiskies before he was allowed to rejoin the wedding party.'

'I'm not saying they've overdone the preparations for this party, but last night I was asked to prepare a toast for the stand-in bride and groom.'

Priests

'There were so many priests at the altar today that I thought we were filming the new sequel to *Men in Black*...'

Public speaking

'Unaccustomed as I am to pubic spanking... er... to public spending... er... to public speaking...'

Qualifications

'Now Dave was very popular at school with the lads, for
his practical jokes and his astonishing footballing skills.
He was pretty popular with the girls' too, as I recall. But on
the qualifications front he didn't fare quite so well. I'm not
saying he's not very academic, but Dave's the only person
I know who's been expelled from the School of Hard Knocks
and sent down from the University of Life. Which was a
great shame, really, as he'd only got in through clearing in
the first place.'

Quotations

'Ladies and gentlemen, it seems to me that a quotation is
a handy thing to have about one, saving one the trouble of
thinking for oneself. [Pause] I think it was AA Milne who
said that. [Pause] In fact, it might even be said that padding
something out with quotations is usually a sign that the
author is afraid to present his own opinions or else is
anxious to show that he is widely read. [Pause] And that
was Philip Bonewits…'

Religion

'A newlywed couple decide to join a church. The vicar tells them, "We'd be delighted to welcome you into our fold. All we ask is that you abstain from sex for two weeks, then come back and see us." Two weeks later they return. "How did it go?" asks the vicar. "Well, not very well," says the husband. "What happened?" asks the vicar. "Well, my wife was reaching up for a packet of cornflakes on the top shelf, and the sight of her stretching excited me so much that I had to make love to her there and then. "Then I'm afraid you won't be welcome in our church," says the vicar. "We're not too popular at the supermarket either," says the man.'

'My courtship with Carole got off to a terrible start when we had a huge row about religion. Of course, I knew she was an Anglican. I just didn't realize about the Archbishop of Canterbury!'

'Tracey has been a believer in reincarnation since way back when… oooh, right back to her mollusc days.'

Research
'When I was preparing this speech, I decided to phone round as many of Cath's friends and family as I could to see what I could find out about her. Yet strangely, no one would return my calls. Finally, I discovered the truth: "You'll get nothing out of me," one tight-lipped girlfriend said. "She's got too much dirt on us as it is."'

Romance
'The other day Mick came up to me with his face all scratched. "What happened?" I asked. "My girlfriend said it with flowers."
"That sounds romantic," I said. "Not really," says Mick. "She shoved a bunch of roses in my face!"'

'Last night I dreamt I was dancing with the most beautiful woman/handsome man in the world. Let me tell you what my wife/husband was wearing.'

'Today's couple are a perfect match. He's blinded by love and she's outta sight!'

'A woman's secret of romantic happiness consists of five easy steps:
1 Find a man who cooks and cleans and know how to mend things.
2 Find a man who makes you laugh.
3 Find a man who's warm, honest, reliable and loves children.
4 Find a man who's a wonderful lover and who satisfies your every need.
5 Make sure that the four of them never meet.'

'Let me give you an idea of how romantic these two are. Every morning, Mick gets up first to make Norma breakfast: a cup of coffee, a croissant and half a fresh grapefruit. "And do you know?" Norma told me. "He even goes to the trouble of removing all the pips from my portion." "That's so romantic," I replied. "Yes it is, I suppose," sighed Norma. "Only I can't stand grapefruit."'

'Deborah and Colin met in the most romantic way, in a little French restaurant. She was sitting at another table when she suddenly started choking on a fishbone. Colin immediately rushed over to her, patted her hard on the back, performed the Heimlich manoeuvre and sorted the problem. Looking at the bone she choked up, he said: "What's a plaice like this doing in a girl like you?"'

'I like to say that Liz and Mike were destined for one another. When they met, she was an occupational therapist specializing in mental health and he... well, he just needed all the help he could get.'

'When Rob summoned up the courage to ask Katherine for a kiss, she said nothing. Well, it's impossible to talk and laugh at the same time, isn't it?'

School days

'I've been lucky enough to obtain... [produce a battered sheaf of paper] one of Jonathan's early school reports. It contains some interesting material that will shed light on the kind of husband Kate can expect him to be. Under Home Economics, for instance, we read: "Always willing to experiment, though rarely so keen on clearing up." Maths? "He enjoys arithmetic, but can't always get everything to add up." Under English, we read: "Capable of great flights of fancy, Jonathan seems at times to be living in a world of his own." And, for Physical Education, it says: "Enthusiastic if rather lacking in technique, Jonathan expends a great deal of energy for very little result."'

'I've no wish to embarrass Rob by harking back to his school days. Besides, I think old "Splatter Knickers" did a pretty good job of that himself already.'

'If you've ever seen the size of Dan in any of his early school photos, you'll know that while he enjoyed his time at St Peter's, these were hardly his salad days. In fact, it was more a case of Hello Mr Chips.'

'When she was 13, Wendy fell heavily in love with Mr Gregory, the geography teacher. To this day she can still recite the annual mean rainfall of Outer Mongolia…'

Second time round
'Many of you may know that this is not my first wedding. But I can categorically assure you that it'll definitely be my last.'

Shoes
'Jane and shoes. Two words. Imelda Marcos.'

Shopping

'Tony and Tina, however well matched, have learnt that the secret of a harmonious relationship is not to go shopping together. Tina likes to spend all day buying one thing, flitting from one shop back to another to compare looks and prices, and buying four pairs of shoes to try on again at home when she only needs one pair. If Tony ruled the world, shops would be open for one hour a day and everyone would have to turn up with a list and say: "I want this, this, this," and be done with it.'

Sporting prowess

'Gareth is so competitive that he has his personal best time for driving to work chalked up on a blackboard in his garage.'

'Gavin is so obsessed with sport that he's got an earpiece tucked in his buttonhole with a direct link to Radio Five Live.'

'Simon prides himself on his fitness levels but he can't even run a bath without getting breathless. Ask him if he's done any exercise this week and he'll say, "Sure: three frames of pool and a round of darts." In fact, he's the only man I know who owns a pair of what he calls "pub trainers".'

'If you've ever wondered what true love is, you only have to watch Janine turning up on a Saturday morning to cheer on Greg as he bats for the local cricket team. Anyone who can sit through that carnage, week in, week out, must be truly devoted. At first she used to shout encouragingly: "Come on, darling!" But now it's: "Just give ME the bat, you plonker!"'

Stag do

'I'd love to tell you how, on his stag night, Steve got a tattoo on his behind, flirted with a seven-foot transvestite, had a brush with the police and woke up on a fishing boat off the coast of Norway. But as usual, he had three pints of light and bitter and crashed out in the corner.'

Star signs

'Neither William nor I really believes in star signs or horoscopes. I know: typical bloody Taureans!'

'When I first met Dave, I couldn't believe that I'd ever fall for him. Sure he was tall, dark and handsome, kind and gentle, with a massive brain and a great sense of humour. But a Piscean!!'

Tears

'Wow, what an emotional service! I know they say that it's good to shed a tear at a wedding, but I've never seen domino-crying on that scale before. Once someone in the first row had gone, the weeping epidemic spread right through the crowd and soon the whole room was awash. Even the organist was splashing great big tears onto her keyboard. I haven't seen anything like that since the great floods of 1992!'

Ticklish

'Having got to know Toby very well over the past 18 months of our courtship, I can tell you that he's got a funny little spot under his chin which, if you tickle it, drives him absolutely mad. I mean livid. And I know he'd just love it if, after the speeches, we all queue up to give his chin a little tickle… [Turn to partner] Wouldn't you dear?'

Touchy

'I wouldn't say Simon's touchy about his receding hairline, but on the stag do he turned down three perfectly good boiled eggs...'

Transport and travel

'Mike thought that Liz was doing all the transport arrangements. How come? Because, he said, she keeps talking about a "wedding train".'

'The other day Harry rang me in a real panic. "How are we going to get to the wedding?" he said. "I'll give you a lift," I replied. "Why, what's the matter?"
"Well, apparently Trish has got her own train," he said.'

'Kerry is such a heavy packer that as we were getting our things together for our honeymoon, I actually had to show her a picture proving that they have kitchen sinks in Sardinia!'

'Why does it take millions of sperm to track down one egg? Because none of them will stop and ask for directions.'

'A man approaches the Mexican border on his bicycle. The guard spots the two large bags he's carrying and asks him what's in them. "Sand," says the cyclist. The guard doesn't believe him, makes him get off his bike and searches him thoroughly. Sure enough, even though he pulls the bags apart, all he can find is sand, so he has to let the cyclist through. Next week, the same thing happens. This time the guard sends the contents of the cyclist's bags off for tests, but the results prove that it's only sand, just as the man says. The same thing happens every week for the next three years: every time the guard searches the man's bags, but turns up only sand. Then one day, off duty, the guard bumps into the cyclist in a bar. "Look," he says. "I won't tell a soul, but I know you're smuggling something. It's driving me mad trying to work it out. Please just tell me what it is so I can sleep again at nights?"
"Bicycles," says the cyclist.'

Upstanding…

'And so, without further ado, let me ask those of you who still can to stand up and join me in a toast…'

'And so will everyone now please raise their glasses – and themselves…'

'And so, in the words of my ex-girlfriend, "I'm going to leave you now."'

Ushers

'If anyone needs assistance at all today, please don't hesitate to call an usher. You can't miss them: they're the ones wearing caps and holding torches…'

'I'd just like to apologize if you were one of the many people my brother-in-law Jack loudly told to "SHUT IT!" during the service. He thinks that's what the usher's job is.'

'Look how smartly turned out all the ushers are today. It's because they've all come straight from court…'

'At a wedding I heard about recently, an usher spotted a man at the back of the church who was sprawled out over three seats. "I must ask you, sir," said the usher politely, "to sit up straight in your place. We need to make space for more guests." The man said nothing, but emitted a loud groan. So the usher repeated his request, but the man merely groaned again. The usher wondered if he was dealing with a random drunk who'd just wandered into the wedding service by accident. So he said: "Please can I ask you, sir, where you've come from?"
"The choir loft," groaned the man.'

'An usher is a bit like the body at an Irish wake. Everyone expects you to be there; but no one expects you to do very much…'

Weather

'The day after Bill met Gwen, he phoned me up and said: "I'm going to get that girl down the aisle, come rain or shine." And, strangely, we've had both today.'

Wedding day

'Of course, today Colette looked wonderfully relaxed and composed throughout the whole ceremony. Not like a wedding I attended recently, where the bride confessed to her maid of honour just beforehand that she was worried she'd completely forget what to do. "You've just got to remember three things," said her friend. "First, walk nice and straight down the aisle. Second, stop and stand when you get to the altar. And, third, sing along with the hymn: it'll relax you." So as the bride arrived at the wedding, she was heard muttering to herself over and over again: "AISLE ALTAR HYMN, AISLE ALTAR HYMN…"'

'But on a serious note, we should be grateful that today is not the wedding day of John Lennon's widow and the lead singer of U2. Otherwise we'd be toasting "Yoko Bono". Or if today were the wedding day of Salvador Dali and Dolly Parton, then we'd be congratulating "Dolly Dali". Then again, imagine if today were the wedding day of Sondra Locke, who had just divorced Elliot Ness so she could marry Herman Munster… and become "Sondra Locke Ness Munster". And what if Woody Allen married Natalie Wood, then left her to marry Gregory Peck, then divorced him to marry Ben Hur? That's right. Today we'd be raising our glasses to none other than… Woody Wood Peck Hur.'

'It's not been easy for Sonia to find a man to share her wedding day with who is warm, caring, funny, well dressed and hygienic. They've nearly all got boyfriends already.'

'During the ceremony today I overheard one little girl say to her mum: "Mummy, Mummy, why is the bride dressed all in white?" Her mum smiled and replied: "Because white is the colour of happiness and today is the happiest day of the bride's life." There was a pause and then the little girl piped up again. "Mummy, Mummy," she said. "Then why is the groom all dressed in black?!"'

'Today's wedding is a love match, pure and simple. She's pure and he's simple.'

'What do you call two spiders that have just got married? Newlywebs.'

'Did you hear about the two bed bugs that were lovers? They got married in the spring.'

'For Susanne, today is the beginning of a whole new era in her life. Many things will be different from now on. In Florida, women who are single, widowed or divorced are not permitted by law to parachute on Sunday afternoons. But, as of today, Susanne can now jump out of a plane over Disneyworld any time she likes…'

'It's lucky Jon wasn't left to organize the big day today. If he had been in charge, the bride and bridesmaids would all have been obliged to wear bikinis, the date of the ceremony would keep changing as Jon tried to avoid any last-minute clashes with sporting events, we'd all be eating buckets of chicken instead of this fine spread, and we'd be toasting the happy couple with magnums of Bud Lite.'

Wedding gifts

'Looking at all the wonderful gifts we've received today, I'm reminded of the story of the couple who got engaged when they were both in their 90s. They went for a stroll to discuss their wedding plans, and wandered into a big chemist's. "Excuse me," asked the couple. "Do you sell heart medication?"

"Yes," said the pharmacist.

"What about rheumatism cream?"

"Oh yes."

"Viagra?"

"Yes, sir."

"Vitamins and sleeping pills?"

"Most certainly."

"Indigestion tablets and denture cleanser?"

"All kinds." The couple looked at each other excitedly. "Are you thinking what I'm thinking?" said the man. "Oh yes," said the woman. So they turned back to the pharmacist and said: "We'd like to have our wedding list here please."'

Wedding gifts

'Ladies and gentlemen, I'd like to thank you for all the many gifts you have so kindly given us today. There they all sit, piled up on that big table over there. I'm glad to say that we haven't received three toasters or fifteen candle sets. I know this already without unwrapping them because, like Darth Vader, I can feel your presents…'

Wedding jitters

'As Martin's father/best friend/best man, let me tell you that he has been so keen for the wedding to go as smoothly as possible – to get hitched without a hitch, so to speak – that he literally turned grey with worry, which is not a good look for a bald man, believe me…'

'I can't help wondering whether Jenny was having second thoughts as we drove over to the church this morning. She kept asking me where reverse was!'

Wedding reception

'Tonight we are lucky enough to have as our DJ, Steve, spinning the platters that matter. Like all official wedding DJs, Steve has a special licence permitting him to play *The Birdie Song/Lady in Red/Agadoo*.'

'Did you hear about the two antennae that got married? Apparently the ceremony wasn't up to much but the reception was terrific.'

Wedding rehearsal

'At a wedding rehearsal, the groom took the priest on one side and offered him £100 if he'd miss out the word "obey" when it came to the "love, honour and obey" bit. The priest nodded and took the cash. But on the day, when it came to the words of the ceremony, the groom was shocked to hear the priest ask him: "Do you promise to grant her every wish, make her breakfast in bed every day and never even look at another woman, so long as you both shall live?"
"Yes," says the groom with a gulp. Afterwards he goes and sees the priest. "I thought we had a deal!" he says accusingly. The priest gives the groom back his £100. "I'm afraid I had a better offer," he replies.'

Wedding service

'An engaged couple met their vicar for a chat about the forthcoming ceremony. The vicar explained that they could choose between a contemporary and a traditional service, and the couple, being young, decided to go contemporary. Come the big day a great storm broke, and on the way to the church the groom had to roll up his trouser legs. But still he managed to reach the church on time and take his place at the altar. As soon as the vicar saw him, he rushed over and hissed: "Pull your trousers down!" The groom gulped and said, "Do you think we could have traditional after all"?'

Whirlwind romance

'It seems incredible that the person I walked down the aisle with today is someone that I didn't even know six months ago. In fact, I had a terrible nightmare that I'd forget Tina's name. But then the best man had a brainwave: If in doubt, just call her "Mrs ___" [say your surname. Pause.]. 'Sorry, not Tina, Julie. I mean Tracey. I mean...'

Who wears the trousers?

'And so, as the one who'll be calling the shots in this marriage… [pause, looks down uncertainly at notes]… at least I think that's what's written down here…'

'In today's ceremony, as you may have noticed, I did not actually say that I would "obey" my new husband. I mean, come on: it's all I can do to respect him…'

Wisdom

'As a father and grandfather who has been happily married for more than three decades, I would like to offer the bride and groom the advice of an old man: "Never go to sleep on a quarrel, never try and whistle with jelly in your mouth, and never eat yellow snow."'

'As a wise person once said: "Take care that your final word in one argument is not the first word of the next one."'

Wives

'If girls are inclined to marry men just like their fathers, is that why so many mothers cry at weddings?'

X-factor

'There was definite chemistry between Mary and Greg from the first day they met. He plied her with dihydrochloride benzylene and she made a beeline for his Leibig condenser.'

'What is the secret chemistry that makes for a wonderful wedding and a loving marriage? Clearly, it's not a formula you can bottle, or someone would have made a fortune from it years ago. But I look at my parents/parents-in-law/grandparents [amend as appropriate], who are still clearly in love with each other to this day, and I say to myself: "I'll have a pint of whatever they're on."'

You're doing it wrong...

'From this list, you can check when you're doing it wrong...

• If the little figures on your wedding cake are wearing overalls.

• If the wedding ceremony has been scheduled to take place during the halftime of a football match.

• If the bridal bouquet has been recycled from a nearby funeral or flowerbed.

• If the morning suits have big football numbers on the back and team logos.

• If a big slobbery labrador has been given the role of best man.

• If, instead of a sit-down spread or buffet, you hand round buckets of chicken pieces.'

Yum, yum

'What a fantastic spread we've enjoyed today. On behalf of everyone, I'd like to say to the cooks/chef/caterers: "Undo me belt, you're nearer."'

Zzzzz...

[Perhaps point at someone who looks like they are a likely candidate for dozing off]

'Of course, in certain cultures it's considered a compliment when a respected guest dozes off during your speech.

[Pull out an enormous bullhorn, gong, bell or similar]

But I don't think that we'll have that problem here, do you?'

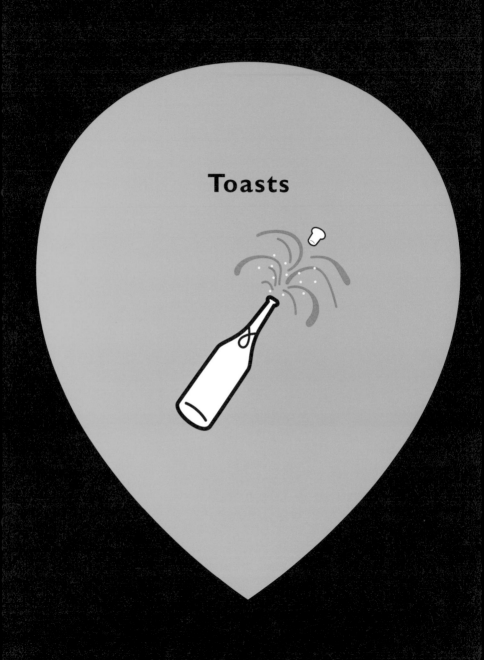

Toasts

Raise your glass! Your essential guide to making toasts.

No wedding would be complete without a toast to the bride and groom, accompanied by a cool sip of bubbly. And today you're likely to be asked to charge your glasses and join in with several other toasts given to and by various members of the wedding party.

Today's increasingly sophisticated wedding speeches have evolved from traditional toasts where guests drank the health of the newlyweds. And although toasts are now often only one element of a larger speech, they still have an important role to play.

At larger, more formal occasions, they provide a natural break in the proceedings that everyone can recognise. And, at smaller, more informal weddings, a beautiful sentiment expressed in a simple toast can be as emotionally charged as a full-on speech. Here we offer advice on making a top toast, together with plenty of sample toasts you can adapt for your own use.

What are toasts for?

Sincerity and practicality are the keys to a successful toast. A toast that comes from the heart will only add to the emotion of an already highly emotional day.

But toasts are of practical value, too. They can help punctuate a day that is always hectic and complicated by alerting guests to the end of speeches, and to the transition from one part of the wedding day to the next.

Toasts should have a clear purpose, whether it's simply to salute the bride and groom (usually the job of the best man) or to honour friends and family who couldn't make it and/or who have passed away.

Toasts can serve as a natural break in the proceedings if – as is often the case with the best man's speech – you have gone through a long list of thank-yous or other messages. And they're a quick and easy way to express additional thanks to specific members of the wedding party, such as the mothers of the bride and groom. If you are presenting gifts during a toast, for instance to the mothers or bridesmaids, make sure you leave time for the exchange to take place.

Rehearsal dinners

Toasts come into their own in the increasingly popular custom of rehearsal dinners. Usually a few days before the wedding, the key players will get together to rehearse the ceremony. This enables the main participants to know what to expect on the day.

In America – and increasingly in the UK – this rehearsal may be followed by a dinner attended by both sets of parents, close friends and anyone who has flown in from afar for the wedding. Very often it's the first time that everyone sitting around the table has been together in years, and it gives the two families a chance to get better acquainted.

During the meal, some or all of those present may be called upon to give a toast.

If you're asked, you may want to share a memory about the bride and groom, or you may want to say something more general about love and marriage. Find inspiration in our sample toasts (pages 108–25).

Traditional toasts

There are no hard and fast rules today, of course, but the order of toasts/speeches traditionally runs as follows: father of the bride, groom and best man.

The father of the bride

Traditionally, the father of the bride makes the first speech or toast, and ends by toasting the bride and groom.

The groom

Traditionally, the groom toasts the bridesmaids/maid of honour. He may also choose to toast his wife, who will then reply and toast the bridesmaids. He may also toast the hosts, his in-laws, especially if there are no bridesmaids.

The best man

Traditionally, the best man ends his speech with a final toast to the happy couple. He may also toast the bride's parents during his speech or 'absent friends' as he reads telegrams/messages from afar.

Other toasts

Increasingly, the bride, and sometimes also the chief bridesmaid will want to say a few words to mark the day. Generally, these toasts will come between those of the groom and best man.

Do's and don'ts

Do instruct the guests as to what to do. For example:
'Please raise your glasses with me…' Give them time
to do so before you launch into the actual toast.

Do tell guests exactly what the wording of the toast is
to be, for example 'To the bride and groom' or 'The happy
couple!' etc. Clarity is the key to a good toast.

Do keep your toast focused.

Do make your toast positive or funny.

Do finish your toast with a flourish and leave them
wanting more.

Do, after the toast, sit when the guests sit down.

Don't rush into a toast before your guests have had time to
follow your instructions or it will end up confused and only
half-heard.

Don't make your toast too wordy – or guests won't be able
to follow it.

Don't forget, where appropriate, to include your partner
in the toast if he/she isn't going to make a speech, for
example 'My wife and I would like to say a special thank
you to the bridesmaids…'

Toasts given by the father of the bride

The father of the bride traditionally toasts the bride and groom at the end of his speech.

Traditional

'I end my speech today by thanking you all for joining us to celebrate the wedding of Annabel and Ben. It's been a wonderful day so far and we hope this will be the beginning of a wonderful life together for them. Please join me in wishing them all the best... To Annabel and Ben!'

Bit of banter

'Before we raise our glasses, John, I'd like you to take Diana's hand and place your own over it. Now remember and cherish this special moment, because believe me, if I know my daughter, this is the last time you'll have the upper hand... To Diana and John!'

Quick quip

'Apparently, my wife tells me, I'm now supposed to make toast. Good grief! Haven't you all eaten enough already? Ah, right, I see, I'm supposed to make a toast. Well, then, please stand and raise your glasses quickly before I mess anything else up and join with me in wishing John and Emma every happiness... To the bride and groom!'

Short and sweet

'Today is all about two people and their decision to spend the rest of their lives together. We wish them good luck and great joy, today and always. So please stand and raise your glasses with me… To the happy couple!'

Getting sentimental

'It's said that when children find true love, parents find true joy — and true joy is what I am feeling today. As a father, whatever else I may have wanted for my children, my abiding wish has always been for them to find relationships in which they can be truly happy. I know Katie has found this with Daniel. Katie, as everyone knows, is the apple of my eye. So for me to say that I have gained a wonderful son-in-law is the greatest compliment that I can give. Ladies and gentlemen, I would like you to join me in drinking a toast to the happy couple. Please be upstanding and raise your glasses to Katie and Daniel.'

Toasts given by the groom

The groom traditionally toasts the bridesmaids/maid of honour. He may also choose to toast his wife, and his wife will then reply and toast the bridesmaids. He may also toast the hosts, traditionally his new in-laws, especially if there are no bridesmaids.

Edible joke

'Apparently, I'm now supposed to toast our hosts, my parents-in-law. That's a bit of a shame because I think I'd rather have them spit-roasted with onions and lots of garlic. Oh, that kind of toast. Awfully sorry, Mr and Mrs Johnson: you know I think you're good enough to eat! To Mr and Mrs Johnson, ladies and gentlemen!'

Thanks, ladies

'I'd like to take this opportunity to thank the bridesmaids for their sterling work. I've discovered that for an occasion like this, you really do need to have experts on table flowers, leg-waxing, eyelash-curling and themed party favours on hand, and Alice, Hannah and Ellen certainly fit the bill. They really have been essential in making this a perfect day. Ladies and gentlemen, please raise your glasses to the bridesmaids.'

One for the parents

'A wedding is a coming together of two families, and I couldn't have wished to join a friendlier family than Stella's, so I'd like to end my speech by thanking our hosts and my new parents-in-law, Betty and Stan, for making this such a wonderful occasion. It's often said that wedding days belong to the happy couple, but there are many people who have helped to make today so perfect. I'd also like to thank my parents, Pauline and Max, for everything they've done for us. Without the hard work of our parents, Stella and I wouldn't have been able to concentrate on having such a good time today! Please raise your glasses to them.'

Love lines

'I'd like to end my speech by proposing a toast to my bride. Without wishing to embarrass anyone by getting too sentimental, Charlotte is all I have ever dreamed of. Someone once said that to love is to receive a glimpse of heaven. Well, I feel I am truly in heaven today… Please raise your glasses to the beautiful bride.'

Toasts given by the best man

The best man traditionally ends his speech with a final toast to the happy couple. He may also toast the hosts (usually the bride's parents) during his speech, and/or 'absent friends' as he reads out messages from those unable to attend.

Beautifully brief

'It gives me tremendous pleasure to propose a toast to the bride and groom. My best friend has found the girl of his dreams and I really couldn't be happier for both of them. Please be upstanding for the bride and groom.'

Joking apart...

'In keeping with tradition, I'd like to say a few words about the happy couple to end my speech. Everyone who knows Paul knows that he likes having his own way, and I've always wondered what kind of woman he'd end up with. Well, Alison is clever and beautiful and, when he met her, Paul, in typical style, let her know who wears the trousers early on. He looked her in the eye and said: "You're the boss!" I knew then that she was the one for him! So please join me in wishing Paul and Alison a wonderful future together.'

A little bit more

'To end my speech I'd like to thank the parents of the
bride and groom for giving us all such a good time. Everyone
involved in this wedding has worked so hard to make it the
great success that it is. I'd also like you to spare a thought
for those friends and family who haven't been able to make
it today. Many of them have sent their good wishes and I'm
sure they're thinking of Julie and Duncan, not to mention the
fabulous spread they're missing! But most of all, I'd like to
propose we drink to Julie and Duncan. It's truly an honour
to be best man at the wedding of such a fantastic couple.
I hope you will join me in wishing them many, many years of
happiness… To the bride and groom.'

Quick quip

'Ladies and gentlemen, please raise your glasses to the
bride and groom. May all their joys be pure joys, and all
their pain Champagne.'

• Find more material for the best man's speech and toast
in our book *The Best Man's Speech*, also in this series.

Toasts given by the bride

Traditionally, the bride does not make a speech, so there is no formal toast for her to make. This means she can choose to toast whomever she likes. Popular choices are her parents/ groom's parents and family, her bridesmaids/helpers, absent friends, particularly if one is a parent or close relative, and/or her new husband!

Poetry in motion

'As I was searching for something to express what I want to say to Rob today, I came across a poem by another Rob, the poet Robert Browning, who wrote: "Grow old along with me! The best is yet to be." I want to thank Rob for agreeing to grow old with me and say that, after such a brilliant day, that if the best is yet to come, I can't wait! So please fill up your glasses and toast my new husband – to Robert!'

Mum's the word

'There's an old Chinese saying that to find a good wife you must look for the daughter of a great mother. After what mum and dad have organized for me today, I think we'll all agree, this is one truly great mother. And Ed and I would like to ask you to make a special toast to thank her. To mum!'

Hard labour

'Many of you might have expected my sister Claire to be my chief bridesmaid and, indeed, that was the original plan. Unfortunately she can't be here today as she's virtually in labour – now what kind of feeble excuse is that? Ladies and gentlemen, please raise your glasses to Claire, the best sister anyone could have.'

Thanks, maids

'I'd like to take this opportunity to thank my lovely bridesmaids for doing my make-up, doing my hair, arranging my bouquet, helping me with my frock and, most importantly, putting up with a complete maniac for the last six months. I promise you, I'll leave you in peace now, girls. Let's drink to them, ladies and gentlemen: The bridesmaids!'

Toasts given by a bridesmaid

Again, bridesmaids don't traditionally toast, so the choice is yours. How about toasting the best man back, or the bride? Then again, there can't really be too many toasts to the happy couple!

Best wishes

'It's not often that the words 'best' and 'man' find their way into one of my sentences, but I think I'll make an exception today! I think we all agree that Jeremy has been an absolute star today – really charming and helpful – and so the bride and groom have asked me to thank him on their behalf, in the hope that he'll remember this when he makes his speech! So please would you stand and toast Jeremy – the best man!'

Best of luck

'I'd like to propose a toast to the happy couple. I honestly can't think of people more suited than Louise and Andrew, and I'd like to take this chance to wish them many happy days ahead. I'd also like to point out to Louise that this is the fourth time I've been bridesmaid, so when you do throw that bouquet – throw it my way! Please raise your glasses to the happy couple.'

Firm friends

'There is no greater honour for any girl than to be asked
to be her friend's bridesmaid, and I want you to know,
Angela, that I was proud to walk down the aisle behind
you today, and that I will always be behind you and Duncan,
ready to support you in whatever way I can. However,
I'm hoping that won't ever mean arranging Duncan's skirt
for him! So can I ask you now to toast with me my beautiful
best friend Angela and her lovely new husband Duncan?
To Angela and Duncan!'

Big sister

'I suppose, as an older sister, I've always been a bit protective
of Nicola – especially where boyfriends were concerned.
In fact, I think I scared quite a few of them off. But in Pete,
Nicky has met a man she can completely trust. Please raise
your glasses to the happy couple, ladies and gentlemen.'

Toasts by purpose

To absent friends (from far away)

Wedding speechmakers might want to mention close
relatives and good friends who can't be there on the day.

'It's wonderful to see so many of our friends and family
gathered here to share Debbie and Ian's happiness. However,
as you know, Shirley and Jim were sadly unable to make it
over from New Zealand to be with us today. They send their
very best wishes to the happy couple, and I'd like to ask you
to charge your glasses and drink a toast to them, and all our
other absent friends. To – absent friends!'

Absence owing to illness

'My Dad's absolutely gutted that he can't be with us today, but, unfortunately, he's languishing in hospital even as we speak. He keeps telling us it's his old war wound playing up, but actually that yoga class finally did for his hip. Anyway, we'll be at his bedside tomorrow with the video to cheer him up, but meanwhile let's raise our glasses to him and other absent friends.'

To absent friends (deceased)

'As you probably all know, I have the honour of speaking in place of Edward, Hayley's father, who passed away last year. All through the day, as I've looked around at everyone having such a great time, I've thought about how much Edward would have loved this wedding. Everyone who knew him will remember how much he enjoyed occasions like this – music, having fun, eating, laughing, having a drink… or two – that was the Ed we all loved. And, of course, he would have been awfully proud and awfully happy to be giving away his beloved daughter. We all miss his presence greatly, but we know that he would have wanted everyone here to have a wonderful time. That's what we intend to do, but first, let's raise our glasses and drink a toast to Edward. Ladies and gentlemen, to Edward, the father and friend we'll never forget.'

Toasts to children

The wedding is bound to be a big occasion in the lives of any children of the bride and/or groom, whether it's cementing their parents' existing relationship or marking the formation of a new family. Make the children feel part of things by offering a toast to them in your speech.

To children (of this relationship)
Lovely bridesmaid
'Of course, this is a very special day for Sam and Georgia, but it's not quite the happiest day of their lives. That day was when their lovely daughter Heather was born and now she's taking part in her parents' big day by being their beautiful bridesmaid. Let's drink a toast to her.'

Baby boom
'Max isn't the only man in Laura's life. There's also their baby son Louis, for whom they're not just the bride and groom, they're the best mum and dad in the world. Will you all join me in raising your glasses to Louis, and may the whole family have many happy days ahead. To Louis and all the family!'

To children (of a previous relationship)
Father figure

'Sarah hasn't just gained a husband in Tom, Leo has also gained a stepdad. Luckily for both of them, Tom shares Leo's love of Curly-Wurlys and computer games, as well as his interest in cars, *Star Wars* films and, more puzzlingly, the fortunes of Manchester City. Here's to many hours of shivering in the stands together – Tom and Leo.'

Mothering matters

'Harry didn't only fall in love with Helen because she's such good fun. He could also see what a great mum she is by the way she has brought up her daughter Alice and son Joe. They are fantastic kids and a real credit to her, so it's not surprising that Harry couldn't stop himself from falling in love with them, too. Now they're all together as one family, and we wish them lots of love- and laugh-filled days to come. So please raise your glasses and drink a toast to Helen and Harry – and Alice and Joe.'

For second marriages

Second marriage speeches can be tricky, so be tactful when you make your toast. Always check your words out with a close family member first.

Voice of experience

'There was once a very famous and successful Avis car rental advertising campaign that simply said: "We're number two. We try harder." Well, this may be marriage number two for this happy couple but, like Avis, they're sure to turn their experience to their advantage. So please raise your glasses to the bride and groom!'

Second chance of happiness

'Sue and Colin are so good together that it's hardly surprising that they've decided to give marriage another try. All weddings are special occasions, but perhaps this one is even more so, because it represents a second chance of happiness for both of them – and they've decided to grab it with both hands. Good luck to them! Please raise your glasses to the happy couple and wish them all the very best for the future. To the happy couple!'

To the happy couple

These examples may help if you're asked to speak at
a wedding where there are no formal speeches, or at a
rehearsal dinner.

'Let's hope that the two of you live as long as you like.
And let's hope you have all you like for as long as you live...'

'I'm a person who likes to use simple words to say simple
things. But before I ask these fine people to raise their
glasses to the happy couple, I'd just like to say:
congratulations on the termination of your isolation. May
I express an appreciation of your determination to end the
desperation and frustration that has caused you so much
consternation. It's such good news that you've been given
inspiration to make a combination to bring an accumulation
to the population. Cheers to the happy couple!'

'I know that, from this day forward, the best days of
your past will be the worst days of your future. Together,
you're going to have the happiest life imaginable. To the
bride and groom!'

'Being a person of very few words, I give you the bride
and groom.'

'Here's to the happy couple. Remember, you two, that you should always view your marriage as if it were a pair of scissors. What I mean by that is that you cannot be separated, even though you're often moving in opposite directions. To the happy couple!'

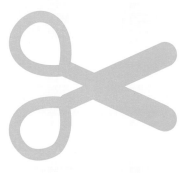

'My advice to the happy couple is to live life as if today is your last day on earth together, and that when tomorrow comes it's simply an added bonus. Here's to today and plenty more bonuses to come – the bride and groom!'

'Just a quick word from me to the bride and groom. Here's to the bride and here's to the groom, all newly wed. May all their troubles be light as bubbles or as feathers that make up their bed!'

'Here's to the newlyweds. Let's just hope that, when push comes to shove, your "for better or for worse" turns out to be far better than worse.'

'Here's to love, laughter and happy ever after. As Rob and Julie start their wedded life, here's to the fabulous new husband and wife.'

'Here's to the health of the bride.
Here's to the health of the groom.
Here's to the ones who tied the knot.
And to the rest of you here, whom I haven't forgot!'

To the parents/grandparents
'Here's to the few who made this crew. To the grandparents!'

'To the greatest grandparents. I've got a feeling that you might be great-grandparents very soon!'

To the bride from the groom
'I'd like you all to fill your glasses and toast Mary, my bride and joy!'

'With every passing day that I've known you, you've got more and more beautiful. But looking at you today, my darling, you already look like tomorrow.'

'Here's to you and here's to me. Let's hope we never disagree. Here's to our families and our honoured guests. And here's to you never wearing those horrid string vests.

Confetti.co.uk is the UK's leading wedding and special occasion website, helping more than 400,000 brides, grooms and guests every month.

Confetti.co.uk is packed full of ideas and advice to help organize every stage of your wedding. At Confetti, you can choose from hundreds of beautiful wedding dresses; investigate our list of more than 3,000 wedding and reception venues; plan your wedding; chat to other brides about their experiences and ask for advice from Aunt Betti our agony aunt. If your guests are online, too, we will even help you set up a wedding website to share details and photos with your family and friends.

Our extensive online content on every aspect of weddings and special occasions is now complemented by our range of books covering every aspect of planning a wedding, for everyone involved. Titles include the complete *Wedding Planner; How to Write a Wedding Speech; The Best Man's Speech; The Best Man's Wedding; The Groom's Wedding; The Father of the Bride's Wedding; Your Daughter's Wedding; Wedding Readings & Vows* and *Wedding Readings*.

Confetti also offer:
Wedding and special occasion stationery – our stunning ranges include all the pieces you will need for all occasions, including christenings, namings, anniversaries and birthday parties.
Wedding and party products – stocking everything you need from streamers to candles to cameras to cards to flowers to fireworks and, of course, confetti!

To find out more or to order your confetti gift book, party brochure or wedding stationery brochure visit: www.confetti.co.uk
call: 0870 840 6060; email: info@confetti.co.uk
visit: Confetti, 80 Tottenham Court Road, London W1T 4TE
or Confetti, The Light, The Headrow, Leeds LS1 8TL